Raspberry Pi

The definitive beginner's guide to understand Raspberry Pi

Table of content

Introduction -

I want to congratulate you for reading this book, it will represent the best source of information about Raspberry Pi. If you want to understand how Raspberry Pi works and get to the next level with your computer, you made the right decision to buy this book.

The world of Raspberry Pi is one that moves fast. With a large active community, new interface boards and software libraries are being developed all the time. So, besides many examples that use specific interface boards or pieces of software, the book also covers basic principles so you can have a better understanding of how to use new technologies that come along as the Raspberry Pi ecosystem develops.

Are you interested in the myriad features of your Raspberry Pi computer? From the hardware to the software? Do you want to understand how you can use your computer at maximum potential?

This book is for you! This book will help you learn how to get the most out of your device.

By the time you finish reading this book, you'll have a firm knowledge of the Raspberry Pi computers and how you can devise your own projects.

Chapter 1- Getting Started with Raspberry Pi

At the end of this chapter you will be:

- In a position to get familiar with the Raspberry Pi
- In a position to know what Raspberry Pi can do for you and how awesome it is
- Knowledgeable on what are Raspberry limitations and how much you can stretch it
- Getting your hands on Raspberry Pi
- Able to know much with regard to Raspberry Pi

Raspberry is one of the most amazing computers developed nowadays. It's a series of small single-board computers. It was originally developed in the United Kingdom by Raspberry Pi Foundation and its main purpose was to promote basic computer science in schools and colleges, after which everything started developing very fast and the original model became far more popular than they anticipated. Raspberry Pi Foundation started selling their original model outside the United Kingdom which was way out of their target market to be used as robotics.

Raspberry being an outstanding invention saw its uptake grow tremendously in that before February 2015 over 5 million units had been sold, not so long they had sold around 11 million units in November 2016, as a result, they became the best-selling British computer company.

A lot of generations have been introduced since the first model of Raspberry Pi model came into the market.

The first model is called Raspberry Pi 1 Model B – the first generation of computers was released in February 2012. It was followed by the Model A, which was lower in price and was simpler than Model B. In 2014 Raspberry Pi Foundation came up with an upgrade with an improved board for Model B called "Raspberry Pi 1 Model B+" which was a great achievement for the company.

The second model is called Raspberry PI 2 – the second generation of computers was released in February 2015 it was an improvement from the first model in terms of added RAM and also an improvement in the design of the product.

The third model is called Raspberry Pi 3 Model B – the third generation of computers was released in February 2016 which came with big improvements like onboard Wi-Fi, Bluetooth and also not to forget about USB boot capabilities. The new model was embraced like the first models, being appreciated for the enhanced features. The latest model out in the market right now it's called Raspberry Pi Zero W having the same functionalities as Raspberry Pi 3 Model B and in addition it's smaller in size, it has a reduced input/output (I/O) and general-purpose input/output (GPIO) capabilities it was released on 28 February 2017 for $10. It's cheap enough that in case it gets broken it will not be a cause for alarm because one can always buy another without a huge financial implication.Being cheap it's one of the biggest advantages of Raspberry Pi.

Let's get familiar with Raspberry Pi!

Lot's of people are excited about Raspberry Pi and its potential. When handling Raspberry Pi for the first time one will easily see that it's a circuit board and has small dimensions the size of a credit card with components and sockets on it.

One can hardly believe that the image above is a full-size computer with enhanced functionalities compared to ordinally computers.We are in the age where most computing devices are still big, shiny, too heavy and not portable enough. Raspberry Pi with its tiny boards it's revolutionizing the computers industry, when one looks at Raspberry Pi you will notice that the boards are transparent, simple and small in size which makes it even more attractive and appealing to most people.With this aspect of reduced dimensions, low price and appealing appearance it's no wonder that Raspberry Pi sold so many units and became so popular in such a short period of time. This is the reward as a result of creating a great product, taking into consideration what people want and delivering exactly according to their ultimate desires.

In a world where everything is becoming more mobile than ever, more powerful than ever and we see the biggest advances in mobile computers, Raspberry Pi made a big step in that direction. The most unusual thing about Raspberry Pi is that it does not run on Windows or Mac OS as you may expect (because they are the most popular operating systems right now). Raspberry Pi runs on an operating system called Linux representing a very different approach to the commercial software industry. Linux as the operating system it's built for companies and volunteers with high skills working together in that one can modify the source code of this operating system, anyone who wants to add some improvements to it can modify the source code and make it how they want. In case you didn't know Linux is an operating system for which one does not have to pay to use it and sharing is allowed as well.

Let's figure out what Raspberry Pi can do!

So let's figure out what Raspberry Pi can do for you! As we talked till now Raspberry Pi it's a fully featured computer and can do anything that a desktop computer can do! Yes, anything that a desktop computer can do, well with little expectations related to the input/output and different ports that you may need for cables and so on.

Even though it has a very low price, it's very accessible for every customer, it's powerful and that one can definitely rely on it as a main computer Raspberry Pi has its own limitations. Raspberry Pi foundation is completely transparent about the performance of a computer using Pentium 2 processors compared to Raspberry Pi. Unfortunately, this computer doesn't have expandable memory, it's pretty limited! The options that you have are the following: 512 MB memory or 256 MB memory.

The Raspberry Pi is definitely not a gaming computer, compared with a gaming console, we can easily compare it with Xbox console released by Microsoft corporations about 10 years ago. So If you are passionate about gaming I would not suggest buying a Raspberry for this purpose. Don't get me wrong the Pentium 2 computers and the first Xbox consoles were incredible pieces of technology for the moment when they were released. But there is a big difference that we have to talk about: the Raspberry Pi it's snappy like crazy! For that period of time, Pentium 2 and Xbox had amazing capabilities and were just incredible for what they did. But even though they are comparable with Raspberry Pi, they are not as snappy as Raspberry Pi is and working as fluid as this machine.

What are the costs for this computer?

When Raspberry Pi Foundation designed this amazing computer they wanted you to have a computer for as low as $25-35 and not to worry too much about its price and how difficult it would be to build a new setup for your office. Let's talk about what you need to build a new setup:

1. Monitor: The monitor is definitely a necessity and you have a couple of options. Due to the fact that Raspberry Pi has a HDMI output, you can connect your computer to a high definition monitor and enjoy a pretty good video quality. Let's say that your monitor doesn't support HDMI, you don't have to worry about that. All you have to do is to check if your monitor has DVI socket and from here all you have to do is just get a cheap adapter for your monitor and connect an HDMI cable to it and you are good to go. A lot of cheap and very good adaptors are in plentiful supply in the market nowadays due to the fact that technology producers are

trying to get things as mobile as possible. My approximation is that in the next 5-10 years almost every computer will be wireless and more portable than now. Wireless charging will be the most needed improvement and upgrade for our personal computers which will bring to an end the need for a charger.

2. FULL HD TV: If you don't have a monitor for your Raspberry PI, don't panic, technology nowadays give us a lot of options. You can get your Raspberry PI connected to a high definition TV using the HDMI socket and you should have a very good experience and enjoy a good quality image.

3. USB Keyboard and Mouse: Good news you don't have to worry about those yellow or violet sockets that you are trying to remember which socket is for the keyboard and which one is for the mouse. The Raspberry Pi works using USB Keyboard and USB mouse so all you have to do is to get a USB equipment.

4. USB HUB: Well, goodbye old adaptors and old sockets. Raspberry Pi comes with one or two USB sockets, depending on the model that you opt for obviously). I strongly suggest buying a powered USB hub for the following reasons:

- You will want also to connect other devices to your computer, you will want to connect your phone, for instance, having just two ports will not let you connect anything else than your keyboard and mouse.
- Having more USB ports will give you more freedom to while using your computer

5. Speakers: Getting some music played is pretty simple. Raspberry Pi comes with a standard audio socket and it's perfect to connect your speakers or your headphones because it uses a 3.5 mm audio jack. You can plug headphones/ speakers directly into it. Just a short note: When using an HDMI connection the audio from your computer will be sent directly to the screen with the video signal and as a result, you won't need separate speakers for that. Keep in mind that this will apply for HDMI NOT a DVI monitor.

6. Computer case: When your first Raspberry Pi comes it will be a motherboard looking very nice, the size of your hand and ready to use. But will have no case. It will be like building a computer from zero but this computer is more simple, more adaptable and mobile than any personal computer that you have ever used. It's wise to get a case for your Raspberry Pi which still makes it attractive.One can buy a plastic one from www.amazon.com or any other site you would prefer. They come in different sizes, colors with and without lead.

As you can see in those 2 images, it just makes your computer look fantastic. It will still have small dimensions and also look great, colored as in the first image or transparent as in the second image and still being at the size of a smartphone or even smaller than that.

7. Power supply: Raspberry Pi uses a Micro USB to connect to power and the good thing is that it's compatible with a lot of phones and tablets out in the market. Basically, you can use your phone to power up your Raspberry. It's worth also checking if you a have a charger, it will be simpler than using your phone, all you need is a charger for your Raspberry Pi and you are good to go. Goodbye long and heavy laptop chargers and worrying about battery life for your laptop. An external battery will also help like the one that you are using for your phone.

Raspberry Pi computers are absolutely great! We can mention also that you can connect USB Keys to your Raspberry Pi (flash drives, to transfer data).Also about storing data like music, pictures and video an external hard drive will be very easy to connect. You will have to connect your hard drive through a powered USB Hub as discussed in the previous point. Computers are becoming more mobile than ever, wireless charging for computers is the next step when we are talking about mobility and I'm pretty sure that we are closer than we think to have that technology in our hands.

Chapter 2: Getting Started with Linux

At the end of this chapter you will:

- Find out about Linux – operating system
- You will know how to use Linux
- Downloading and installing Linux in your Raspberry Pi
- Know how to flash your SD card

Your machine is useless without an operating system, so as a result, you will have to install an operating system on your machine. The operating system allows you to use the main functions of your computer and to rule applications. Linux is the operating system that we are going to use on Raspberry Pi. Other very well known operating systems that we can talk about are Windows and Mac OS.

Let's talk about Linux

Raspberry Pi uses Linux as an operating system, this might be the first time you will be using a Linux computer!

GNU / Linux brings the Linux together with the GNU components and they together create an incredibly simple and complete operating system. Here we have the work of thousands of people that are bringing their efforts into creating something absolutely amazing.

What distribution to use?

You can find distribution for your Raspberry Pi computer on their website *www.raspberrypi.com/downloads*. For any new person in the Linux world and also the Raspberry world I would recommend to you Raspbian Wheezy. This is the version that I recommend because it's optimized for Raspberry Pi by two developers.

Download your Linux distribution it's very simple. But in order to do that, you will have to use another computer to set up the SD card for the installation. Obviously, you will require for that to have a computer (doesn't matter what operating system you use on that computer, Windows, Linux, Mac OS, as long that is functional) and a SD Card, and also internet connection. Go on *www.raspberrypi.com/downloads* get Raspbian Wheezy and:

- Use BitTorrent to download the file
- Use direct download to download the file using your web browser.

Time to flash your SD Card

I hope you have prepared your SD Card and distribution because we are at a very important step. The Linux distribution comes in a special format so it won't be that easy to copy it on your SD card but still a complicated process to do. In order to convert the image file to copy on your SD card, will have to flash the SD CARD.

Flashing your SD Card on Windows it's very simple. "Image Writer" it's the program that we are going to use for this task. It's pretty simple and the good thing is that it's completely free to download.

So let's take a look at the following steps:

1. Download Image Writer *https://launchpad.net/win32-image-writer*. You will need to download the binary file.
2. Extract all files into a folder and open it
3. Start Win32DiskImager.exe. If your computer asks for access, give permission to it
4. Navigate through the Linux distribution .img file and open it. Click on the device menu and chose the drive that contains your SD Card.
5. Click on the Write button and you are good to go

Flashing your SD Card on Mac. Pretty simple to flash a SD Card on Mac. In order to do that we are going to use a script that is called: "RasPiWrite". On Mac, the flashing process is simpler than on Windows so the script will take care even of unzipping the document.

The steps to follow:

1. Download RasPiWrite script and create a folder SD Card Install and subfolder RasPiWrite.
2. Drag all the files from the RasPiWrite folder and move them into the folder that you created
3. Put the Zip file of your Linux distribution into the RaspiWrite folder
4. Press Cmd+Space to laugh your terminal on Mac and search for SD Card Install in the terminal
5. After getting into RasPiWrite folder in the terminal remove any memory cards
6. Insert the SD card in your Mac's SD slot, in case it has or in a card reader
7. Accept questions like "I believe this is your SD card(Y/N)" and now just wait for the process to finish.

Chapter 3 - Connecting your Raspberry Pi

After getting your SD card flashed it's time to connect your Raspberry Pi. Here we have a couple of things that we must take into consideration before starting to connect your Raspberry Pi:

1. We have to insert the SD Card into the Raspberry Pi and install the operating system
2. Connecting your Raspberry Pi to peripheral equipment like monitor/ TV, USB keyboard and mouse, external hard drive, USB Hub, etc.
3. Configure your Raspberry Pi by using Raspi-Config

Even though it might sound pretty complicated actually the rest of the process is very simple. It's as simple as flashing your SD Card like we did earlier and it will be very fun also to connect your Raspberry Pi to the peripheral equipment.

Insert the SD Card into your Raspberry Pi. It's time to start connecting everything, flip your Raspberry Pi over and look under it. You will see the place where you can insert your SD Card and all you have to do is to insert your SD card into your Raspberry Pi.

Next, you will have to connect your Raspberry Pi to a monitor. If your monitor has a HDMI socket you can connect it very easily if not just look for your TV's HDMI socket and you can connect your Raspberry Pi to your TV. USB Hub it's also something very important in what we are doing. Your Raspberry Pi might come with 1 or 2 USB ports, so obviously, more USB ports will be needed. Connect your USB Hub to your Raspberry through the USB port/ports that you have on your Raspberry Pi.

After getting your USB Hub plugged it's time to connect your keyboard and your mouse to your future computer. A number of ports will totally depend on the USB Hub that you chose to buy.

Connect audio to your Raspberry! If you are using a HDMI television the sound will be routed through the HDMI cable to the screen, as a result of that you will not have to worry about connecting a separate audio cable to it. Connecting your headphones to your Raspberry Pi it is also very simple because it has a 3.5 mm audio jack usually situated on the right side of the board, all you have to do is just to plug your headphones or your speakers in case you want louder sound.

Get the internet on your computer! Well, not yet a computer but almost there, we still have a couple of things to set up before calling your Raspberry Pi a computer! Your Raspberry Pi has no network connection on board if is an older model but if it's a newer model it should have an Ethernet socket somewhere on the right side of the board. You can use a socket to connect your Raspberry Pi to an internet router with an Ethernet cable.

Let's turn on your Raspberry Pi for the first time!

What an exciting moment! We flashed our SD card we, got everything plugged now it's the time to turn on our Raspberry Pi for the first time! This will be fun! One more thing that you should take into consideration is the fact that micro USB socket will be on the left (bottom-left) corner of your board and you will connect it to power with a micro USB cable. You will see that your Raspberry Pi doesn't have a button to turn it on and to turn it off. As a result of that when you connect it to power will start working and when you disconnect it will turn off. Pretty simple to use! Be careful to save everything that you are working on your Raspberry Pi computer and I strongly suggest you get a case for your board just to be sure that you are not accidentally removing the power source in the middle of an important project.

Raspi-Config to set up your Raspberry Pi

After turning on your Raspberry Pi computer, the first time you will go into a program called Raspi-Config, which has the purpose of changing the settings of your Raspberry Pi. Now you can use your mouse and your keyboard for the first time.

Here you have the following options:

- Info: to get more information about the tool you are using right now
- Expand_rootfs: Expanding the root partition, here we are talking about your SD card that you flashed earlier
- Overscan: Controls how much of a border should be used around the screen image
- Configure_keyboard: this option it's pretty obvious, it's being used to configure your keyboard with different keys combinations

- Chage_pass: Set's the password for your Raspberry Pi computer. The default password that your computer will come usually is "pi" and the user usually has the same name, "pi".
- Change_locale: We use change_locale to change the language for our Raspberry Pi computer
- Change_timezone: This setting will detect time from the internet and will switch it on, but first you will have to set up your time zone. Also, you will be asked the region where you are right now
- Memory Split: Raspberry Pi has a spitted memory, that means that the memory is shared between the CPU and the graphic card(GPU). Stock distribution allocates 64 MB for the graphic card and the rest for the CPU. This setting enables you to change the split depending on your necessities.
- Overclock: Well overclocking as you may know or not can be done also on your Raspberry Pi computer, this setting allows you to overclock your computer and as a result of that being more faster. However overclocking your Raspberry Pi does not invalidate your warranty so you are safe to do it. Usually Overclocking it's not safe and can put to much stress on your computer and burn your CPU or the component that you are overclocking. Your CPU comes with a speed of 700 MHz stock and has the option to be overclocked to maximum 1000 MHz, obviously depending on the Raspberry Pi model that you have.
- SSH: SSH is being used to secure your computer and to set up security between multiple computers and the settings that you have let you enable or disable this options.
- Boot_behaviour: Let's your computer to go directly to desktop when you turn it on. Kind of a "sleep mode" like you have on Windows computers
- Update: This setting lets you to update to another Raspi-Config when it's available. If you just flashed your SD card you should have available the newest Raspi-Config version.

When you are done with configuring your Raspberry Pi computer just press finish and congratulations! You just configured your computer and now you can use it! Booting for the first time will be interesting! You will be asked for a username and also a password for your brand new computer. The username and password if not asked may come default as "pi" for both.

Note: Don't forget to get a case for your computer! Keep in mind that your board it's pretty fragile and also will be easier for you to use it when it's being protected.

Chapter 4 - Using the desktop environment

In this chapter we will talk about:

- How to navigate and use the desktop
- How Linux actually works
- Browsing the web and how to manage files
- Customization and protecting for your Linux
- And much, much more!

We got to the point where we have access to our desktop, now we can start costuming our computer, working, browsing the internet, programming, storing personal files and much more. If it's the first time when you are using Linux, don't worry, you will get used to it pretty fast. Linux it's simple to use, has a very friendly interface and you will enjoy using Linux a lot. In this chapter we get you through the desktop environment and introduce you to this operating system.

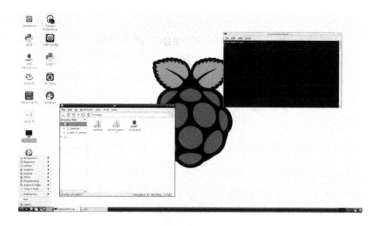

As you can see in the image above, looks pretty simple and familiar with the operating systems that you may have used before. Linux it's not an old or outdated operating system, it's just different, just another operating system like any other operating system. Looks more like Windows if we had to compare to a well known operating system on the market. It has the icons on the desktop and a start menu with all your options.

Le's talk about a couple of icons that we have on the desktop! Your operating system will come with a couple of preinstalled apps that will help you navigate through the system.

Scratch: a simple programming language that helps you because it's very easy to use and learn and approachable by people of any age.

Pi Store: Well as the name says it's the store created by Raspberry Pi foundation to go and download free and paid apps that you might need

IDLE 3: It's used by those who are programming in Python

LXTerminal: Opens a command line, the purpose is for resolving any type of problem with leaving the desktop.

Wi-Fi Config: It's an application that you can use to set up your Wi-Fi connection and get the internet on your computer.

The Start Menu

You will see applications on your desktop and also the "start menu".

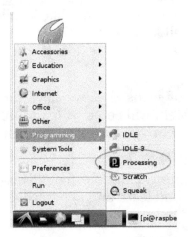

Well as I said at the start of the chapter the desktop environment of Linux looks a lot like Windows and also behaves in many ways like Windows. In the lower part of the screen, you may have the menu that has different categories like accessories, education, graphics, the internet and so on. You can access any of this to work and have access either from desktop environment either from the start menu.

Multiple desktops

You can have multiple desktops while using your computer that can be pretty useful when you need a lot of visual space to display all the information's that you are working with. You can have double the amount of space that you need to work in and all that with two desktops on your monitor. Also RESIZING and closing your windows it's made almost like on Windows in any LXDE session. The controls for any window are very simple and displayed in the upper right corner:

- X button in top right corner of the application has the purpose to close the windows that are currently opened
- The Maximize button is in the middle of the three options its purpose is to enlarge the application so that it fills the whole screen.
- The Minimize button puts down or "hides" the window that you currently have opened but doesn't stop it from running.

It's pretty simple also to change the size of any window, just move the mouse cursor to one of the edges until the mouse icon changes and then click and resize the window by dragging.

Task Manager

Task Manager is also available in Linux, you can use it in case your Linux doesn't work anymore or crashes. Task Manager is represented as a bar chart that scrolls from right to left and shows you the latest information.

Let's talk about File Manager

The File Manager is the equivalent of My computer on Windows. You can use File Manger to see all your documents in one place like music, photos, applications, documents and any other personal information. You can delete, install, move and rename any application that you have and you will see that it's pretty similar to the Windows experience.

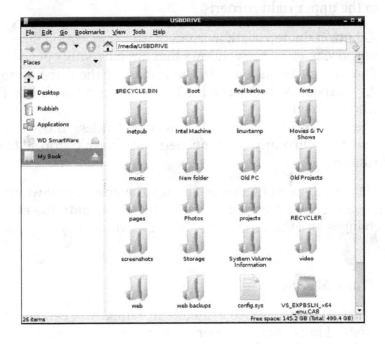

As you can see on the left side of the window there are a couple of "Places" that are available. Any place has the option to

Add tabs, to go to the previous folder, next folder, history folder, home, the "current path" and also a close button to close the window you are currently in.

Let's start navigating through the **file manager.** Each file that you are seeing on the screen of your computer indicates what type of file is. As you can see in the image above there are different types of files. By double clicking on a folder, you can open it. By using right click will bring an option called "Open with".

On your Raspberry Pi computer there are four types of folders:

1. The Pi folder: this is the folder that has most of your files, documents and photos stored. The Pi folder is the only folder that you have on your computer that gives you access to editing and also writing files as an ordinary user.
2. The Desktop folder: is the folder that shows you the programs and files that are on the desktop right now.
3. The Rubbish folder : the rubbish folder it's the equivalent of recycle bin on Windows. You can add files that you want to delete in this specific folder, it's also used as a "temporary place" to put the documents that you want to delete. It's very simple to empty the "trash" all you have to do it's just right-clicking on the folder and chose to restore it as before.
4. The Applications folder: it's a folder that will give you access to programs that you use as "Program menu" does, it's just an alternative that you have for quicker access to your programs.

Now that we have an idea about the types of folders that we have let's take a look at the following. Across the top of the File Manager, we have a couple of options that we are going to talk about. They are a couple of simple shortcuts, frequently used, also found in many operating systems and really common in operating systems world:

1. Add Tab: If you have used an operating system before probably you are conversant with this shortcut. Windows, Mac, Linux doesn't matter what operating system we are talking about right now. Tabs are very useful when working with lots of windows and want quick access to different folders. Having the option to add a new tab will help you a lot to switch between different folders or if you are on the web it will help you to work with multiple web pages.
2. Next Folder: "Next Folder" it's the options that enable you to access the next folder that you have without closing the current folder. "Next Folder" enables you to go forward through your history and to do as often as you need when working or just simply browsing your computer.
3. Previous Folder: As "Next Folder" it's an option that you have to use and to navigate through folders back and forth, very useful for quick access.
4. History Folder: as the name suggests, will let you have access to your history of folders. You can click on it and have access to multiple folders that you navigated and go specifically to that folder without clicking "Previous Folder" till you find that particular folder. It makes searching through folders really easy.
5. Home: The "Home" button it's a button with a very clear and simple purpose. The "Home" button will take you back to the Pi folder and in this way, you will have quick access to the main folder.
6. Path: The path, like in other operating systems enables you to write the location of the folder that you want to have access to. It's similar to the "Path" on Windows and use the same method to navigate.

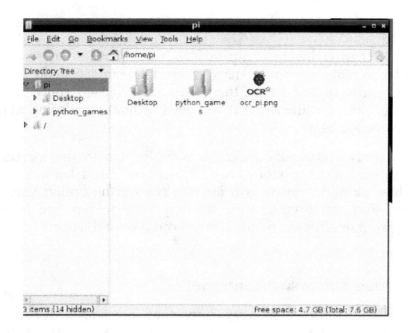

Select folder to move them:

As we have discussed you can be able to delete, copy or even move folders at the same time (When you right-click on a file a menu will appear with all the options that we have talked about i.e to rename the file, delete it and many other options). Here are the ways you can delete, copy or move files at the same time:

1. Hold the CTRL Key and click each file in turn to select them
2. Click with the mouse on the background of File Manager and drag the mouse over all folders

Create a new folder

When trying to organize files it's important to create a folder to make easy to manage them. You can see easily what files you have and where they are saved then go you can go straight to a specific file that you need without wondering as to where to locate it.

It is pretty easy to create a folder. Go to the location where you want to store your information. On a blank space right-click and a menu will appear, choose the option Create New. You can even change the way your folders are being displayed or after the name, size or even type of the document.

Let's browse the internet

The Internet is very important nowadays. It's very important to have access to the internet when working and probably your work is based on some browsing activity on the web. Either you are using your Raspberry Pi computer at work for your company or working at home for the personal purpose I'm pretty sure that the work that you are doing will require in one way or another access to the internet for browsing in either case you will require data or an application with an internet connection. You should not worry about internet connection due to the fact that we have resolved that part when preparing your Raspberry Pi computer. When it comes to choosing a browser your computer comes with 3 web browsers, and we are going to talk about each browser and its capabilities.

1. Midori: it's a simple browser, "lightweight" browser that supports JavaScript. It's created to handle simple sites and offers an easy browsing experience. Big websites like Apple's website or Twitter website it's possible to handle them but a little bit slower than you are used to with the rest of the browsers.

   Features:

- Integration with GTK+ 2 and GTK+ 3 support
- Tabs, windows and session management
- Configurable web search
- User scripts and user styles support
- Bookmark management
- Customizable and extensible interface
- Extension modules can be written in C
- Supports HTML 5
- DuckDuckGo as a default search engine
- Internationalized domain names support
- Smart Bookmarks
- Extensions

2. Dillo : This is a very fast browser for your Raspberry Pi computer that i totally recommend you to use as your main browser. It's fast, simple and can handle very easily any type of website that you are thinking of it loads very quickly. You will notice that the web pages look a little bit different on this browser than you may expect. This browser can't handle JavaScript. It's a very good choice if you are browsing on web for simple websites or text websites having more informational content than visual content.

"Features of Dillo include bookmarks, tabbed browsing, and support for JPEG, PNG (including alpha transparency), and GIF images. Partial support for CSS was introduced in release 2.1. Settings such as the default fonts, background color, downloads folder, and home page are customizable through configuration files. Cookies are supported but disabled by default due to privacy concerns. While most web browsers retain the web cache and history after the program is closed, Dillo automatically clears them to improve both privacy and performance." Source: Wikipedia.com

3. Netsurf: Netsurf it's a browser that can be used for more advanced tasks. This browser doesn't support JavaScript and it looks like out of those three browsers just Midori supports JavaScript for handling interactive web pages. Bye bye to Facebook addiction in case you are a Facebook addicted this is due to the fact that this website can't handle it.

Features

NetSurf's multi-platform core is written in ANSI C and implements most of the HTML 4 and CSS 2.1 specifications using its own bespoke layout engine. As of version 2.0, NetSurf uses *Hubbub*, an HTML parser that follows the HTML5 specification. As well as rendering GIF, JPEG, PNG and BMP images, the browser also supports formats native to RISC OS, including Sprite, Draw and ArtWorks files.

Those are the 3 main browsers that you will find on a Raspberry Pi computer when you start using it. Let's go a little bit deeper into the web talk.

Midori Web Browser

We are going to use Midori For an example purposes and for the fact that it supports JavaScript. To start using Midori you have to go to Programs menu or you can double-click on the icon of the browser that may be on the desktop of your computer.

A page will be opened, probably the homepage of your browser and you will see a very basic browser, with an address bar, like in any other browser, with a New Tab button, Back and Forward button, Reload and so on.

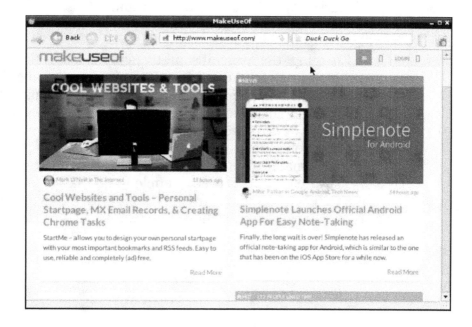

As you can see in the image above it looks exactly like any other browser. The default search engine in Midori is Duck Duck Go, a very popular search engine on Linux and Raspberry Pi computers. Duck Duck Go it's a search engine that is supposed not to track your behavior on the web. Most search engines nowadays are tracking your behavior on the web and here we are talking mainly about Google, Bing or Yahoo   Duck Duck Go promises to give you suggestions to your web pages without tracking your behavior, interesting, I know.

Add bookmarks! It's pretty simple to add bookmarks to your browser and to visit them later. All you have to do is to click on Add Bookmark button and a window will open showing you a couple of options that you have before saving that web page like Title that you want to add to your bookmark, address, folder, the possibility to show in the toolbar and also the option to run as web application.

Zooming the page it's pretty simple also! Normal features we are referring to about Zooming are opening the web page in full screen and also magnifications. Just use CTRL + the mouse's scroll wheel to zoom in and to zoom out. If you want to protect your privacy then you should know that your browser stores history of your web pages. When information has been saved on your computer you can easily delete it. It's pretty simple to do that, as on any other web browser you have the option to Clear Private Data from the menu on the upper part of the browser on the right side.

Image Viewer

When viewing photos on your computer you will probably use LXDE (comes with your Linux when you install it). Among that accessory that you have in your "Programs menu" is an application called Image Viewer and we are going to talk a little bit more about it.

Let's talk about a couple of buttons that we have here:

- Previous: As the name suggests by clicking it you are going to the previous photo
- Next: Sends you to the next photo, you can also use arrow keys on your keyboard.
- Start Slideshow: By clicking this button you will start a slideshow of your photos that are being selected in that folder
- Zoom in/ out: Zoom in enables you to increase the magnification of the photo, zoom into and out of the photo thus reducing or increasing the magnification of the photo.
- Fit Image to Window: This button shrinks a large image and in this way it makes it fit in the Image Viewer
- Go to original size: This button simply resets the zooming options that have been applied to the image and reverts the image to the original size. It even has a shortcut on the keyboard on the letter G.
- Full Screen: Pretty obvious what this button does, by

pressing this button your image will fill the monitor and it will be on the whole screen. The shortcut for this option is the key F11 on your keyboard.

- Rotate left/right: Rotate left rotates the image at 90 degrees and rotate right also rotates at 90 degrees in the opposite direction.
- Open file: This button enables you to open a folder to add a new image or if you don't want to use this button to add a new image you can simply click on the image and drag it.
- Save file: A very well known button enables you to save the image you had opened or to replace the original. It has a shortcut and the key for the shortcut is the key S on the keyboard.

Leafpad Text Editor

When it comes to text editors Leafpad is the recommendation that I have for you. It's a simple text that can be used for writing, text editing, working on documents and any activities related to text creation. It's useful for editing documents and web pages. It's very simple to use and to start new documents to print file and so on.

Customization on your desktop can be made with different styles, different colors(like on Windows), you also have a Widget tab. On the color tab, you have the option to chose your own color scheme based on your preferences. Also, the taskbar that is located at the bottom of your screen has the option to be customized, all you have to do is to right-click on it and go to Panel Preferences located at the bottom of the menu. Any change that you make in Panel preferences can be made without having to save and confirm, you just select what you want to change. For changing the desktop wallpaper right-click on the background and go to Desktop Preferences.

When you are done working I suggest you log out from LXDE and then re-log again when you start working. To log out just click on the red power off icon that is located on the lower side of the screen and then clicks Logout. After that, all you have to do is just confirm that you want to log out and that's all.

Chapter 5 - Using the Linux Shell

In this chapter will talk about:

- What is Linux file system and how to use it
- Basic and advanced commands to use
- How to start creating directories and how to browse for files
- What is required to install software in your Linux Shell
- How many accounts can you have on your Raspberry Pi and how to manage your accounts
- Tricks on how to customize your shell and much more!

You might have had some past experiences with Linux shell, if not and it's the first time you will discover that it uses commands, it's a text – based way of communicating instructions to your computer and requires a little exercise to understand. After getting comfortable with the commands you will feel like using Linux Shell is one of the easiest things in the world.

When you turned on your Raspberry Pi computer you probably saw the shell, usually, it's the first thing that you see when starting your computer. Shell is a name derived from "Bash" an acronym from Bourne Again Shell. The original purpose was to replace the Bourne shell. Bash is used on the majority of Linux distributions.

We are going to discuss more how to use the shell, its advantages, different commands that you can use and why it's a good idea to learn how to use the shell.

Before starting working on shell we have to log in first, but very important, don't type "startx". This will get you into the desktop environment. But if you have typed "startx" and you already are in the desktop environment, just double click LX Terminal icon and a window will appear to start a shell session.

Understand how the Prompt works

pi@raspberrypi ~ $ it will be the first thing that you are going to see. This is prompt and it will be ready for you to enter your command.

pi@raspberrypi ~ $ Looks pretty complicated, to be honest, and I'm pretty sure that you also have the same notion. All it represents is that " Ok you can start entering commands to execute them" that's mostly what the prompt says. Let's take a deeper look at the prompt and discuss a couple of very important points:

- Pi: From the start, I want to specify that this will represent the name of the user that is logged in. You can add a different user to your Raspberry Pi computer and also you can log in as a different user
- Raspberry Pi: Well Raspberrypi is the hostname of the machine that you are currently working with right now, other computers (on the different operating system) use different names to identify the machine when it's connecting.
- ~: The tilde symbol is related to the way files are being organized in Linux. This is a little bit different because in general files are being organized in "directories" not folders. ~ tells you that directory that you are looking at currently(we are talking about home directory).
- $: a Final symbol that we are using is the dollar sign and it's related to the type of user that you are. $ it's being used for ordinary users, not a power user. A super user will see a "#" instead of "$" it's an indication of the type of permissions that you have.

Change directories and check files type

Directories have the color blue and there are two main types of results that you can have: desktop and python_games. To change the directory that you are currently in you have to enter the command "cd" with the name of the directory and then press enter and it should look something like this:

pi@raspberrypi ~ $ cd python_games

Now we have changed the directory and the prompt will show you the directory that you have changed after the ~ symbol and you can also check if the directory has been changed.

Having the freedom to change the directory is essential otherwise working with Linux shell would not be possible. You may want to check the type of a particular file. The "file" command is the command that will tell you more about the type of the file that you are working with right now. After you enter the command name just put the name of the file that you want to find out more information about and a list of information will appear after you press enter. The "file" command will tell you a lot of information about the file that you are interested in if it's an image or an audio recording, what is the size of the image in pixels, in case it's a photo, the type of video and so on.

Parent Directory

So far we have been talking about how to find out the directory you are in, information about the file that you are working on and how you can start working with the Linux shell. We are going to discuss now how to change the parent directory. Often you will find yourself in a situation where you have to switch to the parent directory. To change the parent directory you will have to use two dots after "cd" command. For example:

pi@raspberrypi ~ /python_games $ cd ..

pi@raspberrypi ~ $

The ~ it's just a shorthand to your home directory. As mentioned above the ~ has the same name as your username and usually comes by default "pi" on your computer.

Directory Tree

We have come to a point where we have to get a better understanding of the directory tree. A directory tree is just a metaphor for the way the directories are being organized inside your computer. Think about the metaphor in the following way, a tree has branches, some of them are having secondary branches and so on. Like a tree that has many branches so is your Raspberry Pi computer that has only one root directory and that root directory has more directories that come under it (they are called subdirectories and have subdirectories inside them) like the branches of the tree. You can also think of it as a map. Your root directory has 20 directories under it. All your programs, information, files and operating system data are stored there, it's the location where your Raspberry Pi stores everything.

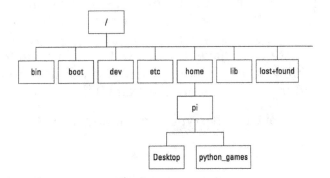

Let's take a look at the main directories that you can use on your Linux computer.

Bin: it's the short form for "binaries" and the bin directory has just mainly small programs and behaves like commands in the shell.

Boot: This directory contains the Linux kernel, here it's the "brain" or "heart" of the system if you wouldn't have a boot directory your Raspberry Pi won't work. The boot directory contains configuration files and stores a lot of technical settings for your Raspberry Pi computer.

Dev: The dev directory has the purpose of storing a list of devices like network connections that your computer can understand to work with.

Etc: Etc directory has the purpose of storing different configuration files that can be applied to all users on that computer.

Home: this is not the first encounter with the home directory, as you may know now the purpose of the home directory is to keep a directory of each user and also this directory can write and store files by default.

Lib: As the name suggests, lib, it's a folder that store libraries, to be more specific that means shared programs and they are being used by different operating system programs.

Lost+found: A very useful directory.This directory is used when the file system gets corrupted or infected and it has the purpose to recover the system(partially).

Media: This directory deals with removable storage devices like Memory Sticks

Root: This directory is reserved for the root user, which is a power user. Raspberry Pi doesn't advise you to use the root account it advises to use "sudo" for the same purpose.

Sbin: Reserved for the root user

Sys: This directory is for Linux operating system files

Tmp: As the name says is for temporary files

Usr: It is used for files for ordinary users

Var: This directory holds data that has variable size

Relative and absolute paths

Absolute paths usually originate from down the root and they start with a / and list the directories that you want you are interested in. As an example, the path to the pi directory is /home/pi.

Cd/home pi / Desktop - If you want to go to desktop directory

cd /- If you want to go root

cd ~ - If you want another directory that's inside your home directory

A relative path refers to a subdirectory that is below the current one and just lists the path through the subdirectories in order.

Let's investigate a little more about options for ls commands

- -1 = Adding a number and outputs the results in a single column instead of a row
- -a = Displays all files including hidden files
- -F = Puts a symbol beside a filename to indicate it's type
- -h = This option expresses file sizes using kilobytes, megabytes, gigabytes
- -l = Displays results in the long format and shows permissions of files
- -m = Lists the results separated by commas
- -R = this is a recursive option that opens any subdirectories and lists and their results too
- -r = the reverse option that displays results in reverse order
- -S = this option sorts the results by their size
- -t = this option sorts the results after their date and time when they were last modified
- -X = sorts after the file extension

Creating directories

To create a directory it's very easy, you have to use the next command: mkdir. You can even use this command to create multiple directories like this :

pi@raspberrypi ~$ mkdir work for today

Deleting from Linux

To delete files from your Linux computer you have to use the command rm, representing the short form for remove. Pay attention because there is no option to recover files from recycle bin, once deleted it will be deleted from your Linux. The rm command is used in the following way: rm work file.

Copying files on Linux

To copy or to rename a file is pretty simple like any other command on your Linux computer, the command is cp and it looks like these:

Cp [option] copy_form copy_to

.

See what's installed on your computer

Dpkg –list is the command that you have to use, it doesn't need root authority to run.

Conclusion

Thank you again for downloading this book!

I hope this book was able to help you to understand how to work with Raspberry Pi and how to use your computer.

The next step is to be sure that you fully understand the information, also apply it and read it as frequently as necessary.

Finally, if you enjoyed this book, then I'd like to ask you for a favour, would you be kind enough to leave a review for this book on Amazon? It'd be greatly appreciated!

If you enjoyed the the this book check out other releases that you might like:

Data Analytics: Essentials to master Data Analytics and get your business to the next level